written by
HEMANTA PATI

ADHYYAN BOOKS

© **Hemanta Pati**

A Gift of Passion

1st Edition

All rights reserved

Publication Date: December 2018

Price: ₹299 | $9.99

ISBN: 978-93-87502-14-7

Published by:

Adhyyan Books

Office No. 637,

Opposite Vivanta by Taj,

DDA SFS. Pocket-1, Dwarka,

Sec-22, New Delhi-110077, India

Website: http://adhyyanbooks.com

E-mail: contact@adhyyanbooks.com

Every effort has been made to avoid errors or omissions in this publication. In spite of this, errors may creep in. Any mistake, error or discrepancy noted may be brought to our notice which shall be taken care of in the next edition. It is notified that neither the publisher nor the author or seller will be taken responsible for any damage or loss of action to any one, of any kind, in any manner, therefrom. It is suggested that to avoid any doubt the reader should cross-check all the facts, law and contents of the publication with original Government publication or notifications.

No part of this book may be reproduced or copied in any form or by any mean [graphic, electronic or mechanical, including photocopying, recording, taping, or information retrieval systems] or reproduced on any disc tape, perforated media or other information storage device, etc., without the written permission of the author. Breach of this condition is liable for legal action.

For binding mistake, misprints or for missing pages, etc., the publisher's liability is limited to replacement within one month of purchase by similar edition. All expenses in this connection are to be borne by the purchaser.

All disputes are subject to Delhi jurisdiction only.

Dedicated to my Mother

Foreword

There is difference between "being seen as a success" and "feeling like a success." I was hooked on this line and kept on pondering over the differences between the two. Hemanta takes you through a very strong perspective on the difference between the two.

Ask any long distance runner, he or she has that hidden dream or a wish in the bucket list to be called as an Ultra Marathoner. A brilliant built up comparing stages of life akin to the ultra marathon of 75km which he ran. Liked the way author pauses between mile stone mileages in the race and goes back to his growing up and the career building days.

Focus on the social status which is a prebuilt notion and the pressure peers put on us, with the depth of this line Hemanta has put in a great perspective about passion vs reality to survive in the life as is seen in the society by the people who are the so called guardian of this society.

Somehow when we move in to the next echelons of life, we want to see the passion, we wanted to live, through our kids and we visualize - it's through them we see us.

Have we lived our passion or are we imposing our passion on our kids? Do we still pursue our passion at any age? Trust me being a passionate runner, I can vouch for it that age is just a number; passion knew no time, ignite the fire or for that matter ensure that the fire kept igniting.

Author has defined aptly through this line:

"When the feelings of self-identity are not through your passion, the fear of failure will always relegate your passion and keep you engaged in finding and holding on to your hypocritical identity"

In search of the livelihood and a better tomorrow which is as per the society norms, we tend to kill our passion.

It is very important to have your family on your side and for them to support the madness you are pursuing.

It is also important to balance out. If you are reasonable in your approach and allocate the right amount of time to your career and passion, you need not have such fear of loss. Alternatively, if you are going all out on your passion, the fear of loss is genuine, but it is worth taking the risk, but again we are predominantly from the cultural chords of Indian Society and the society somehow restricts us , because we too fear for the social standings .

I am so happy to see that author found his balance and also reignite the passion which he had left in the memory lanes. His two important passions for sports and writing were prominent from childhood. I would like to mention on how he got up at 2 am to complete a run and catch a flight at 6 am. That shows how serious and passionate he is about his love for running. One line which impressed me was how the author in the due course of time became "planned me" from "Circumstantial me".

Author gifted himself both of his passions at the later stage in the life. What a beautiful comparison about his 1st Passion and 2nd Passion, running and writing through the stages of marathon.

Never compromise on your passion, if it can't form main stream in your life still pursue it, may be someday your passion will be the reason to keep you motivated and make your life exciting.

Wishing Hemanta, all the best.

Lt Cdr Bijay Nair, (Retd)

Marathoner, Ex Indian Naval Officer and Author of #TheyInspire

Preface

The world is full of successful people.

Success is a relative phenomenon and anybody who feels successful has his/her own definition of it.

In the crowd of successful individuals there are people who have defined 2 sides of success: 1) Success as seen by others and 2) Success as felt by self.

There is difference between "being seen as a success" and "feeling like a success".

You may be tempted to call it hypocrisy.

However, there are many underlying forces that work to give rise to such a state and many individuals inadvertently relegate the importance of "feeling like a success" to the oblivion and try to accept the accolades that come from the environment out of "seeing him/her as successful".

Every individual wants to feel the success but very few get the opportunity to do so.

The question is "Can an individual work toward feeling the success?"

Those who can feel the success are **happy and contented people**.

I have tried to relate my life's journey so far toward a contented me. The journey of my life is symbolic and the references to running and writing a book can be replaced with the reader's passions.

It could be anybody's life.

Contents

Foreword	*vii*
Preface	*xi*
1. The BIG DREAM-The Ultra Marathon	1
2. The Flag Off	9
3. The First Break at the 10 Km Mark	15
4. End of the Trail at the 20 km Mark	23
5. The Climb up is Over	29
6. Ran Beyond the Full Marathon Distance	35
7. Only 20 km More… I was Excited…	43
8. Final Sprint to Realization of My Dream	55
9. The Finish Line of the Dream Ultra Marathon	67
Epilogue	*81*

CHAPTER 1
The BIG DREAM- The Ultra Marathon

On the Starting Line

It was November 11, 2017, and I was standing at the starting line of an Ultra Marathon that would cover a distance of 75 Kilometers. This one will bring me full circle from 10K, 15K, 21K, 25K, 28K, 32K, 42k, and now 75k. The thought of covering a distance beyond a full marathon was raising so many questions in my head. Considering the level of endurance required, there were only a handful of fellow runners who were concentrating on their warm-ups and stretches. The briefing was being given by the race director regarding the route, aid stations, timing recording, and the markers on the route.

The run will take a lot out of me in terms of physical and mental stress.

How did I get there? What brought me to this?

Instead of getting into the regular warm-ups and stretches before the run I, in my subconscious state of mind, started searching for the answers. There was another 20 minutes time left before the flag off for the run and I, a 53-year-old runner, started recounting all that led me to stand at the starting line of an Ultra Marathon, probably a 10 to 11-hour grind along the road, trail, and hills.

When I Reached 50 Years of Age

Where was I?

(a) A High-Profile Designation?

One fine morning I woke up to a tinkle on my mobile. The tinkle was from the office mailbox and I clicked on the new mail. The mail read "Effective April 1, 2017, the company has decided to re-designate various levels in the company." I quickly ran down the table of designations – old and new- and found myself upgraded from VP to Sr. VP! I was happy and called my wife to share the news. I had fallen to rise again. For example, when I left the PSU job to venture into a private sector job, I took a huge risk. I needed a different skill set to manage my job in the private sector. It took me some time to acquire the required skills and, in the meantime, I handled the job with the new skills. It required a lot of self-discipline and the driving force was the need to support my family and to pay for my son's education. But the question was, "Was I enjoying this?"

(b) Good Pay?

The pay is important. You need it to provide a better life for your loved ones and a better education for your children. I was no different. I burned the midnight oil to succeed in the job for a better pay. It is as if you are running for your life, and the survival instinct got me to the level where I am now. At present, the pay is reasonable. I could provide a decent education for my son. I fulfilled all my social responsibilities (family responsibilities).

(c) A Posh Apartment?

The need for my own roof over my head was strong enough for me to work hard and earn that bit extra to own a house. Initially, the requirement was to have a house in my home town. However, I couldn't make ends meet and be able to generate the extra bit I needed to go for it. The employer's housing loan offer was too conservative even to go for a house in a smaller city. However, the urge to have a house was strong and made me combine my housing loan and my wife's to go for a house in my home town. After buying that house, we thought that we were done in terms of house-buying.

In 2001, the insurance industry opened up to private

players and the only experienced manpower pool was available in the PSU Company where I was working. The opportunities were there for a quantum jump in income right from day one with private insurance companies. This temptation to change jobs had strong roots due to the paltry income in the PSU job. First, my wife and then I ventured into the risky private sector. More disposable income was there and over a period of time that resulted in having 2 more houses in a couple of other cities in addition to the one we owned in my home town. The urge to have more houses was realized, some through loans and some through savings.

(d) A Better Car?

Though the job in the PSU had a perquisite of a car, it was limited to few brands such as Maruti/Fiat. It took 9 years in the PSU Company for me to be able to afford a car, which was a Maruti 800. It brought with it the responsibilities of a sales job in the Life Insurance Industry, people who know the domain will vouch for its difficulty. The shift to private sector 6 years thereafter provided the luxury of having a sedan and a better brand, Ford. Having jumped into the pool, you have to swim either to save your life or to enjoy the swimming. Probably, in my case it is the first one. The never-ending desire for material things was on an upward trend, not only due to the comfort that I wanted but also due to the expectations from society (you may read it as vanity; I wanted to show and justify that all was well with me). That has landed me with 2 better cars-one for us (my wife and I) and other for my son.

(e) Social Status?

My schooling was from a small rural school in Odisha and in a radius of 6 to 7 Kilometers there were 4 high schools including the one I had attended. The so-called good students at these schools knew each other and competed among themselves. I was one among them. From my school in the year 1980, there were 3 guys including me who passed in first division in the state board examinations. If we include the other 3 high schools, there were approximately 10 or 12 students who achieved first division. The seniors in the area always had very high expectations of us without realizing the fact that there were bigger competitions outside. I remember when I did not do well in the Intermediate Science examinations and was forced to change to Humanities to graduate, elderly well-wishers in my area started questioning my future. My social status got a dent then. Of course my answer to those questions then was "the journey has just started and it has not ended, let's wait till the end". People laughed at me. The repair work started when I graduated from a less-known college in Odisha. The urge to bounce back was strong and I achieved a rare First Class with Distinction in Economics Honors and was admitted to the premier PG class at the University at Bhubaneswar. Thereafter, my slogan was "if not Civil Services then Bank PO or AAO in LIC/GIC is a certainty". Exactly that happened and here I am in the Life Insurance Industry. Many of the senior people who were questioning my capability in my town then have disappeared. The expectations of your environment play an important role in your growth and choice (forced) of career and hence social status.

(f) Am I Hypocritical?

When I sit back calmly over a cup of tea in the evening after coming back from the office and I think of all that happened, I feel happy. My deep analysis of the status was triggered one day when with such a cup of tea I traveled down memory lane to the past and thought about my son.

My son, who is doing his final year B Tech (IT) now, was 11 years old then. He was studying 5th standard. He was mad about computers then. We were staying in rented premises at Salt Lake in Kolkata which was very close to the Cricket Coaching Academy of Sourav Ganguly. Right from my childhood, I have been an ardent follower of sports. I always dreamed to be a sports person and take up sports as a career.

One day, I decided to send my son to Sourav Ganguly Academy of Cricket. Daily I would take him to the academy and wait there to pick him up. One month passed. One day driving back home from the Cricket Academy my son asked, "Papa, why do you want to impose your passion/ dream on me by asking me to play cricket? I have heard you and mummy discussing the fact that you wanted to be a sports person. But I don't share the same passion."

I then decided he didn't need to go to the Academy anymore.

I allowed him to pursue his own passion.

The remembrance was nostalgic. It raised few questions that I had not thought of before.

- What about me then?
- Was I pursuing my passion?
- Did I do enough to stay with my passion?
- If my son could realize the fact at the age of 11, why couldn't I?

I tried to travel further down memory lane as far back in the past as possible. I stumbled upon a sweet memory when, at the age of 14, my friend and I cycled 45 kms early in the morning to play a cricket match and came cycling back in the evening.

Another memory was about playing a match the day before my graduation examination. After taking guard for the first ball, I looked up and I saw my elder brother standing near the sight screen. I remember, how much I prayed not to get out before my brother left.

In rural schools those days, there was no concept of a school magazine. I along with few of my friends initiated a handwritten school magazine to help our passion for writing poems and short stories.

These early passions gave way to the hard reality of a

middle-class status and the need to do well in academics and get a well-paying job. A first class in Economics Honors and a post-graduation in Applied Economics saw me through to the highest entry level job in the Life Insurance Industry in India. Thereafter, the rat race for doing well in the job and getting a promotion continued.

Remembering these memories and the underlying happiness proves that I am hypocritical while I say I am successful and happy today with a high-profile job, high pay, a high-end car, and a fine apartment. In the deep corner somewhere in my heart , still, the sports person or the writer is searching for an outlet to give me happiness which is real!

I don't blame the job which meets the necessities of my life, my family, and my responsibilities. I blame myself for not giving voice to my passions in my life.

Now, almost at the twilight of my career (I mean the job which I am doing) I am realizing the fact that I did nothing for my passions which were so dear to me during my formative days in school and college.

They say it is never too late and age is just a number.

CHAPTER 2
The Flag Off

In the meantime, the clock at the start line gate indicated that the time of flag off is a few seconds away. The countdown started 10, 9, 8, 7, ... 1 and the chatter-patter of the shoes of the runners hitting the tar road started. Over the last 3 years I have got conditioned to this sound and I started to put one foot in front of the other and moved ahead along with the crowd of the runners. This being a distance more than a full marathon, the plan was to take the start very easy and conserve the energy for the entire grind of 10 to 11 hours. While getting into a slow rhythm for the next 10 kilometers (I had decided to take a small break at the 10 K point) I again slipped back down memory lane and tried to explore who I was by the time I was 50 years of age.

When I Passed 50 Years

Who Was I?

(a) An Individual?

I was traveling from Delhi to Mumbai on my way back from an official trip. The flight was at 5 pm, and I reached the boarding gate only 15 minutes before take-off. The gate was closed. I requested the airline staff to allow me board the flight. The question was asked, "Who are you?" My natural reaction to that question was, "I am a traveler, and have booked a ticket on the said flight." So, how did I identify myself as at that counter? "I am a traveler with a valid ticket!" (a micro view of myself at that point of time). If I were asked the same question just now what would be my answer? "I am an individual, a human being in God's creation" (a macro view of myself). My identity is one of a few billion such human beings who are treading this planet at this point of time.

(b) A Son?

If I come out of the macro view and answer the same question, the first thought would be to identify myself with my parents. My parents gave me life and I am their son. I have a host of responsibilities toward them. They have done so many things in bringing me up and making me capable of performing the various activities which I am able to do now. Hence, I do have an obligation to live their dream. Every parent becomes pleased when they see their children become successful. The definition of a child's success for a parent is based on their experience of success and that may not match that of the child. Still, as a son, I have to be happy that my parents feel that I have become successful having a white collared PSU job and climbing up the professional ladder. According to my parents, I am a successful son.

(c) A Husband?

This is an identification of social responsibility. You are a spouse (if married) and your other half identifies you as husband or wife. I feel that my wife considers me a successful husband based on various parameters, such as job, earnings, handling the family responsibilities, and meeting social responsibilities. The marriage is 24-years-old and our bond is growing stronger. We perfectly complement each other. During the last 24 years of marriage, due to career considerations we have been separated almost 13 years. That's one thing we have had to compromise for the so-called career, and still we are very close to each other. I will fail in my duty if I only say a successful husband; rather we are a successful couple.

(d) A Father?

I do consider myself extremely lucky to have my son Ankit. He is doing his final year B. Tech. in IT now. He is a wizard in coding and aspires for only a career in that domain. From his birth until today, he has not got the advantage of his Papa. When he was born at Bhubaneswar, I was at Madras and saw him for the first time when he was 2 months old as I was busy in FY closing work. I had to leave him when he was 3 years old due to a transfer to a marketing assignment in LIC and could only rejoin him when he was 5 years old. After 2 years, my wife decided to join the private sector and was posted to a different city and I had to stay back. In this way, Ankit's entire formative years were neglected by my absence leaving my wife to take on all the responsibilities. I strongly feel that I have not done justice to him. I missed being with him when he was growing up. I would not rate myself a successful father at all.

(e) A Friend?

It is said that an individual can be better judged from the circle of friends he keeps. It is a choice as far as having a friend is concerned. I have friends from my school days who are still connected to me. Few of my college friends are in touch though they have chosen various careers. The friends I made during the initial training days in LIC are a strong group of around hundred individuals and we are still in touch. In the last 13 years in the private sector, I have made purposeful acquaintances but not friends except few good friends. A few of my friends have also moved to the private sector; a few are in the same organization where I am, and we are still friends. While climbing up the ladder in the corporate hierarchy, I have tried my best not to hurt any of my friends in the process. I am happy to subscribe to this ideology though it did not help me climb faster but it helped me to be able to sleep peacefully every night. I have a few friends and the bond is very strong.

(f) A Samaritan?

While I completed my studies, striving for success never left any space for the activities of a Samaritan. After my studies, the race to find a job, and providing the best possible living for my family took precedence over any social service activity. I enjoyed success in the job, my bank balance, and the social recognition associated with it. Upon introspection, I feel whatever I did till I was 50 was because of some perceived responsibility and it was not out of my own passion. The happiness involved in my work, success, and recognition is a hypocrisy. A Samaritan can't be hypocritical in his attitude or activity.

(g) An Angel?

No, I have not done anything to qualify me as an angel, But, somewhere in the deepest corner of my heart an angel lives, always fighting with and subdued by the identity crisis. . *When the feelings of self identity are not through your passion, the fear of failure will always relegate your passion and keep you engaged in finding and holding on to your hypocritical identity.* That's what happened to me from my formative years until I was more than 50.

CHAPTER 3
The First Break at the 10 Km Mark

The experience over the last 3 years of running was sufficient to see me through the first 10 kilometers comfortably. It took 75 minutes at a very slow pace of around 7mins. 30sec. per kilometer. The cadence of around 160 to 170 was a cakewalk for me, but the consciousness of the fact that it was a distance of 75 kilometers was haunting me. The search for the answers to the questions kept me engaged in my subconscious mind through the first 10 km of the run so much so that I ignored the waves and cheers from some of the fellow runners and volunteers along the way. Up to the 10 km, mark it was a tar road which was mostly flat. The organizers had informed us that the segment of the route from 10 km to 20 km mark will be a rolling trail in a jungle and there were direction markings and we must look for those to navigate through the trail. After taking water and energy gels during the short break, I started into the trail segment. The path was uneven and the thick cover of trees was keeping the sunlight away. The atmosphere was cool and comfortable for the run. Considering the uneven path, I decided to cover the next 10 km in 80 minutes and I got into a rhythm of around 8mins/kilometer. I did not worry about a few runners overtaking me. While running a long-distance, as an amateur, the competition should be ignored and you are supposed to compete with your own self.. As I had not run such a distance before, I did not have a benchmark to compete against. I was into a very comfortable pace and rhythm. The subconscious again got engaged in finding the answers to those questions....

Searching for my Childhood

What Was My Passion?

(a) What attracted me in my formative years?

One day recently and by accident, I met one of my seniors in school who had appreciated my sportsmanship and he was dissatisfied to know my present status and he expected that I would have chosen sports as my career.

My formative years were spent in a typical village setting. The family structure was a joint family. Sharing and caring was in the blood. My childhood saw a transition from abject poverty to middle-class and my family was education-conscious. The seniors in my joint family understood the importance of education. In a typical village upper-primary school, I was introduced to an education which was a combination of book education and physical activity through unorganized village sports. As a child, I had a huge inclination toward physical games and used to bunk school to play with my friends whose families were not so serious about education, quite unlike my family. The primary education was in the hands of few angel-like teachers who always felt that it was their responsibility to provide me with a good educational foundation.

I graduated to high school which was just a kilometer away from my village, and in the school, my family had the reputation of doing well in academics. All my brothers and sisters who passed out of that school had done well in the board exams. Seeing my inclination to sports and games, the teachers started telling me the stories of the success of my elder siblings in academics and advised me to concentrate on my studies. The clash between my inner passion for sports and the external advice from teachers put a lot of pressure on my mind. The advice of the teachers, then, were like lines from the Bible and I followed them. The child in me sometimes rebelled and took me out for games and sports, oblivious of the fact that I would get flak from teachers and seniors. I would ride a borrowed bicycle with my friend for 45 kms early in the morning to play a cricket match and return in the evening on a Sunday only to face a barrage of questions and reprimands.

The concentration on studies started molding me and I unintentionally became interested in writing thanks to my English literature teacher. I thought of publishing a school magazine and discussed this with one of my teachers who appreciated the idea. However, the economic condition of the school and students were not at all conducive for this activity. My teacher and I decided to prepare a handwritten magazine and few of my classmates agreed to help write copy. We decided to publish 20 copies of the magazine which would be designed and handwritten by us. The name was aptly given "SADHANA." I took the lead in collecting the articles and writings from students and editing them. We took pains in writing the 20 copies and designing the cover by hand. We did all this without the knowledge of our class teacher and our Head Master.

The day came to show our work to our class teacher. I was excited and expected that we will be appreciated by our teacher. To our surprise and disappointment, we were cold- shouldered, and not allowed to continue and we were not able to fathom the logic.

We were dejected. Going against the wishes of our teachers then was unthinkable. Afterwards, our HM who was godly man allowed us to publish a few of the selected articles and writings on a wall magazine with the same name as "SADHANA." To my surprise, my article did not qualify to be published. The writer in me was nipped in the bud.

Two of my passions which were very prominent during my formative days in school were sports and writing.

(b) What was my dream?

Unlike the present generation, the dreams of a student in a rural school in the late 70s were not as prominent or defined. But I was always attracted to physical activities, games, and sports. After doing reasonably well in the board exams in 1980, I was admitted to the Intermediate Science course in college. While in college, a little freedom again drifted me toward my passion for sports and I started devoting my time to play cricket, though the economic condition did not allow me to have my own cricketing kit. Borrowed bats, pads, and gloves helped me play at the college level. The passion drove me to arrange village-level cricket tournaments. My friend and I would use the moon light to draw the lime powder boundary on the cricket field where we arranged the first tournament in our area. "These guys have gone mad," people said. My dream was to be a cricketer.

(c) When did I start diluting my dream?

All the activities during the 2 years of Intermediate Science caused me to drift away from studies and I didn't do well in the course. Everything was blamed on my passion for cricket. Family members looked down on me. I did not get admission into a good college for the graduation course.

I somehow managed to be admitted to the Economics Honors course in a little-known college in rural Cuttack District. With only 5 students, the classes there were boring. I knew I will have to do well and graduate to get a seat in the PG classes at the University. My fellow students in the college discouraged me by saying "Anybody doing Economics Honors from this college could not dare to get a seat in University PG classes." I thought, as far as my career is concerned, everything was lost…

The cricket team selection for the Inter-College Cricket Tournament started. Having known that my career had hit a wall in this college, I participated in the selection nets and got through to the college team to open the innings in the inter-college matches. I played a few matches and as the college team was not strong enough, we were knocked out of the tournament in the second round. I did not see a great future in cricket from this college either.

The family had lost all hopes of me doing well in academics.

Under the circumstances, I had only one door to knock on, which was self-study to graduate. I decided to talk to the Head of the Department. He was a dynamic man, and after listening to my predicament, he agreed to help me understand a few difficult lessons in economics, and also waived my attendance requirements.

Thereafter, I did not attend classes; I stayed back in the hostel and studied on my own. It was April 1985, the final exams were to start on Monday, and I was studying as if there were no tomorrow. It was Saturday and a few friends from the local cricket club knocked my door. They invited me to play a cricket match on Sunday, just a day before the exams. My passion was ignited; temptation took precedence over the exams. I was blind to everything else. I agreed. It was a police ground and I walked onto the batting crease, took the guard and with an opener's stance looked up to face the first ball. A current of guilt traveled down my veins when I saw my elder brother standing nearer to the sight screen. I did not know whether he realized that I was there. I prayed not to leave before he left the grounds. I knew he was a busy banker and he would not stand there long despite his interest in the game. Thank GOD, I carried my bat through the innings.

Exams passed reasonably well. To my surprise, I got a First Class with distinction and qualified for a seat in PG classes at the University.

The University was full of academics. I got involved in the race to qualify for a good job. The influence of all the students competing for a white-collar job, matched the expectations of my family and my passions for cricket and writing were sacrificed at the altar of those lucrative white-collar jobs.

During my University days, though I played some cricket matches organized by the PG council of the University, they were not going to lead anywhere to get into competitive cricket. Besides, the age to play was disappearing.

I did well in PG final exams and well enough to secure a white-collar PSU job.

The dream of becoming a cricketer ended and cricket, for me, became a pastime activity.

(d) How I compromised

If I reminisce, I find that drifting away from my passion cannot be blamed only on circumstances. I, as an individual, was responsible. Many times I read stories about many people coming from a similar back ground to mine and doing great in their respective passions. Maybe, I didn't have sufficient courage to challenge the status quo.

CHAPTER 4
End of the Trail at the 20 km Mark

Before this run, I had done a trail run in Mount Abu 2 years ago. This trail was different. Keeping in the right direction was a challenge. I missed the markers a couple of times and the volunteers helped. In the process, I ran an additional 1.5 km. The target of finishing the trail segment in 80 minutes was extended to 93 minutes. This was a first-time experience. I was irritated when I realized that I had to run 1.5 km more than necessary. Though there was route support from the organizers, I was prepared with some food and an energy drink in my backpack. I utilized the short break to take some light food and few sips of energy drink and collected my breath. The next segment of the route was around 15 kilometers which involved a few steep hills to be negotiated up and down. As I had lost 13 minutes in the last 10 km, I decided to make up

5 minutes in this segment. I planned to cover the next 15 km in 115 minutes instead of 120 minutes. Running an Ultra Marathon really requires careful planning of the entire journey: the pace during each segment, the breaks, the food, the medical checkups, and energy supplements. For an amateur like me, it is the finish that is important rather than the timing of the finish. My break was over and it was time to start again. The legs were little tired. I told myself, "Hey, you can't complain of tired legs after 20 kms of a 75 km run. You must not involve your legs for running. You should run from your core." It was a good reminder and I concentrated on the involvement of core muscles and started into the next leg of the run. The first steep gradient was after 2 km and as advised by senior runners, I decided to negotiate the next 3 km of the upward run with smaller strides, lifting the knee, leaning forward, rhythmic arm movements, and avoiding walking. As I started the climb with short strides and got into the rhythm, my subconscious again got into the act of searching for the answers to the questions…

The Fight Against the Self

The Inhibitions

(a) Is it the time now?

The realization has come to me. I have become hypocritical about the so-called success I have achieved. So what if I have realized it? Can I mend it now? I am standing almost at the twilight of my working life or at the start of the countdown (10, 9, 8, …). Do I have enough time to salvage something? I was saddled with all these questions when I realized that I had not done justice to my passion, regardless of the excuses I invented to justify it. (*Humans are the only animals who can justify all their deeds.*) I decided not to justify but to rectify. The question of time still remained. My passion was sports. I am 50 plus and I can't win an Olympic Medal or get onto an Indian cricket team. Maybe I will only have another 10 or15 years of active life and is that enough?

(b) Point of no return

My life had been decided over 24 years of my working life, and it is very difficult to decide to do something new; even thinking of it is difficult! I know only Insurance Sales numbers, ways to sell, ways to direct a sales team to achieve sales numbers, earning bonuses, qualifying for a trip abroad, addressing a meeting, preparing an attractive sales presentation and so on… I have developed a bear-belly with a sedentary life style. Walking down the lane is even becoming difficult. I have reached a state where physical activity for sports is an alien thought. This is the "Point of No Return" and it comes to everyone who realizes the fact and decides to change. Emerging from this "Point of No Return" stage is difficult but not impossible.

(c) Social stigma

Someone with gray hair, wrinkled skin, and weak muscles

decides to train for a sport which he has not done ever before causes people to raise eyebrows. Skeptical remarks are made. People make fun of you. Many of us older, out-of-shape individuals feel this stigma while doing something which does not perceptually fit our age. There are examples of people who ignore the social stigma and do what they perceive as correct. There is a community developing now in society that supports breaking perceptual barriers. Today, if you do something that does not conform to the perceived rule, different groups will either 1) oppose you, 2) jeer at you, 3) encourage you, or 4) support you.

With the discouragement & opposition you may stop, or with the encouragement and support you may continue toward something against the normal perception. *Which one should you choose?*

\Social Stigma is a Myth now-a-days for those who dare to do.

(d) Family Acceptance?

I don't give a damn about anything else as long as people who matter to me are ok with what I do. In India, the acceptance of the family is a very important motivation. At the age of 50+, you suddenly decide to wake up one morning and set out to train for sports as if you are going to win an Olympic Medal. How does your spouse react? How about your children? How do your old parents react? How does your neighbor react? There may be acceptance, rejection, or constructive criticism. I must say it is very important to have your family on your side for such type of madness.

(e) Fear of Loss

I am having a successful career, good job, and reasonable social recognition. If I follow my passion at this late stage with sincerity I may have to sacrifice all or many of them. I may not do justice to the job which I may lose while following my passion. I may lose my social recognition attached with my job. There will be a financial loss. All these thoughts can pin you down while deciding to follow your passion at a late age. However, there is a myth around this fear. If you are reasonable in your approach and manage time for your career and passion, you need not have such fear..

(f) Self-Doubt

Doubt is a dangerous phenomenon in human psychology. It, in its various forms, has created havoc in human existence since times immemorial. The most dangerous of the manifestations of doubt is self-doubt. If you doubt your abilities, then you are nowhere. Either you know you can do or you know you can't do. There is no in between in the form of doubt. Before doing anything, you need to evaluate your capabilities which are in your control and be sure of it. This will solve 90% of your problems of a project.

CHAPTER 5
The Climb up is Over

The last 15 km of the route was really tough as it involved steep and unending inclines. The experience of doing some tough hill runs such as Bopdev Ghat LoSM run, Arey Forest Run, Mount Abu Half Marathon, and the Satara Hill Half Marathon really helped me negotiate those inclines. The time I took for this segment was 109 minutes as opposed to my plan of 115 minutes. It was a "Wow!" feeling. I thought this was possible because of a few downhill segments where I was going too fast. The realization came when I felt a little pain on my knee. It is a fact that the downhill run needs more care as it puts a lot of strain on the knees. The faster the pace, the more strain on the knees. I took out the route plan from my backpack and checked the next 40 km route. The next 40 K involved 2 or 3 moderate uphill climbs and rest was flat. I thought my knee could sustain it. I took out the knee cap from the backpack and put it on my left knee. I took one energy gel and sipped some water. My planned break was for 5 minutes and after doing few static stretches, I decided to start again. The dream of running an Ultra Marathon was becoming reality. Whenever I had broached the topic running an Ultra Marathon, I was reprimanded by my wife. However, after she accompanied me to 2 tough runs, such as Durshet Forest Marathon (32 km) and Satara Hill Half Marathon, her resistance disappeared. She knew that I know my limits and I would listen to my body and take care. In addition, by this time, she knew it would be very difficult to stop me from running the races I plan to. The next 10 km involved a few moderate uphill climbs & I was up for it. I had planned a moderate time target of 80 minutes for next 10 km. My break was over, and I began to run. After few hundred meters, the subconscious again got into that act of searching for answers…

Opportunities and the Grab

The Courage

(a) The Incident

There are many small and big incidents which happen in every individual's day-to-day life. Some are obviously significant and catch our attention and some are ignored. A keen observation of all the incidents with the benefit of hindsight will tell you that the incident, though insignificant, can change your perspective greatly. An incident happened in my life in 2014. I sought a transfer to Mumbai from Kolkata to be nearer to my family at Pune. I was posted to a non-sales job at Head Office, Mumbai. Obviously, coming from a high-pressure sales job, the assignment at HO gave me little more "me time." But that's not the incident I am talking about. In the month of October, 2014, I received mail from my company's corporate communication team asking for my participation in SCMM 2015 in various race categories which were to be sponsored by the company. Being a morning walker, I hesitated. Thanks to my friend Mr. Yogesh Shrivastava, he motivated me to participate in the Half Marathon category. After agreeing to participate in the Half Marathon category in SCMM 2015, I started to test my limits of endurance by running longer distances in the mornings. Many times I came close to quitting.

Small incidents provide a huge opportunity- you need to grab it.

(b) How I broke the barriers

Practicing the run in the morning at Mumbai is a huge issue. If you are late in the morning, the monstrous traffic will be a huge obstacle and it is almost impossible to wade through the traffic. Hence, you need to get up very early in the morning. As they say, you have to be a '4 am-er' to practice running on the Mumbai roads. That was the first barrier – getting up at 4 am. With the alarm set at 3.45 am, I had to come out of bed to stop the ringing alarm and that would break the barrier of wanting to sleep a little longer.

The other mental barrier was, "what would people think of me if I go for a practice run at the 50+ age?" Many times this haunted me. Once, while surfing the internet for the running communities in Mumbai, I stumbled upon few runners who were 60 years and more in age. There were many in my age group also. I realized, "I am not alone in this craziness, there are many more." *We try to confirm our action by checking if anybody else does what we do.* I stopped worrying. I was really happy that I was doing something that was in sync with my passion for sports. The happiness was showing in my expressions. Many of my colleagues who were close to me realized that I was happier.

We can achieve better results if we come out of this mindset of finding a precedent for everything we try to do. Why can't we be the first one to do something innovative?

(c) Where was the help?

While practicing my runs in the morning I felt that I needed somebody who could advise me on the nuances of long-distance running, but I was not mentally ready to hire a coach. This was partly because of the expense involved and partly because of the fear of failure. The information available on the internet helped me a lot. Many experts give valuable tips on running for the beginners. I utilized such advice and improved my cadence, landing, breathing, and control of heart-rate while running. Information is at your fingertips and if the activity is a passion for you, nobody can stop you from getting help.

Go out and follow your passion in an informed way...

(d) What Ifs

While practicing every morning, a barrage of questions used to come up in my mind regarding the activities I was doing to actualize my passion for sports:

1. Am I doing the right thing?
2. What if I am unable to finish the Half Marathon?
3. What if I finish the Half Marathon?
4. What next? I mean what to do after the SCMM 2015?

One fact I was sure of was that the practice of morning runs was a healthy thing and was keeping me fresh all through the day. If I didn't finish the SCMM 2015, my passion was strong enough to go for the next one with more practice. If I could finish this one, I would go for more such events. After a month's practice, I was aware of so many events that were happening on a regular basis across the country and I could participate in those after SCMM 2015.

The quicker the answer to all iffy questions, the better it is.

(e) Can I realign myself?

The daily morning run of around 1 and a half hours kept me fresh all through the day, required me to hit the bed at 10 pm sharp for the next morning wake up at 3.45 am. This was contrary to my regular routine of going to bed after midnight. The TV and social media time needed to be cut. It was a challenge, but my passion was strong enough. I could realign myself. I finished my office work in time daily so that I got back home early. The weekend travel to meet my family was managed in such a way that not a single morning run was compromised. I changed my eating habits by increasing the protein intake to take care of muscle wear and tear due to running. The pre-run carb-loading also was a part of the change in eating habits.

The will to realign in favor of your passion is important.

(a) Can my family realign?

The support of the family was important for such realignment. I had a detailed discussion with my wife regarding this and she was all for my passion. She knew that I was always interested in sports and games, but she cautioned against overdoing it. Until I called her from the finish line of SCMM 2015 after finishing the HM in 2 hours and 17 minutes, she had some doubt about all this. After that, she never questioned my resolve and supported me all the way.

If you are honest in your endeavor and passion the support will be there from all corners.

CHAPTER 6
Ran Beyond the Full Marathon Distance

The beep on my Garmin indicated the completion of the 45 km. The volunteers on the aid station were smiling and cheering and offering bananas, chikkies, and water. The feeling of running beyond the full marathon distance for the first time was awesome. A sense of victory was clearly visible on my face. The volunteers at the aid station reinforced the confidence by saying, "You can do it, 30 more kilometers." The last 10 km was moderately tough due to the elevations it presented. I had taken exactly 80 minutes as planned. Now, the next 30 kilometers are flat, serpentine tracks through the fields and the villages. My energy levels had depleted, legs were tired & body needed rest. The tug-of-war between body and mind was at the peak. I stopped and looked for a doctor at the aid station to have a checkup of my vital health parameters. ....All was well.

I took a banana and a little bit of water. A few sips of energy drink, and the planned break of 5 minutes was over. I decided to break the next 30 Kilometers into 3 smaller segments each of 10 km. By this time, I had been running for 6 hour and 21 minutes. The next 30 kilometers need to be completed in 3 hours and 39 minutes if I was to finish the race in 10 hours and 10 hours was reasonable considering the fact that I was a first-time Ultra Marathoner. I took solace from the fact that I had completed the tough 32K Durshet Forest Marathon in 3 hours and 43 minutes a couple months ago. I told myself, "Hey, you can complete it in within 10 hours." There was a lot of self-talk during a long run. Again, my inner voice confronted me and made me aware of the fact that the Durshet 32 km was on fresh legs and this 30 km would be on tired legs which have already moved incessantly for last 6 hours and 21 minutes.

I told myself, "Don't think much about the 30 km, just think of the next 10 km, and set a target to complete it in 75 minutes."

I took off from the aid station. The next 10 km stretch was going to be a target-oriented one. I had decided to do it in 75 minutes. After getting into the comfort zone of a rhythmic pace of 7 minutes 30 seconds per km, I slipped into memory lane once again…

The Preparations ...

The New ME

(a) Have I decided "Enough is Enough"?

Two months after I started my practice for SCMM 2015, I was traveling to Delhi on a business trip. I was to catch a very early morning flight at 6 am. The night before, I was thinking how to have the morning run as I would have to start for the airport at 4 am. I was in no mood to compromise either the office work—my profession—or the morning run—my passion. I decided, I will do both with the same determination. I got up at 2 am and went for a run for one hour and then prepared myself to catch the flight. And this became the routine whenever I had an early morning flight.

Work is my bread and butter, but at the same time my real passion must get its share too.

I was seeing an inkling of a "New ME" at the end of the tunnel...

(b) What did I do?

After deciding to take my passion further post the SCMM 2015, I registered for the Thane Half Marathon in February, 2015, Bangalore Half Marathon in September, 2015, Delhi Half Marathon in November, 2015, and Pune Half Marathon in December, 2015. In order to prepare for these runs, my daily average practice run increased from 5 kilometers to 10 kilometers. My endurance started to increase. I felt at ease running daily long distances. The Facebook groups of runners kept motivating and appreciating the practice runs as well as organized race performances. The runners high, the state of happiness due to endorphin secretion in the brain because of long-distance running that I got from completing these half marathons were multiplying. Each time I ran the half marathon, I felt that I was doing meditation in motion. I was not looking at the time in which I was completing these runs. The aim was to complete these races and crave for the runners high at the end of each race. In the Mumbai Running Circuit, I was recognized as one of the regular runners.

(c) **What are the steps?**

Following my passion had become an addiction. The normal Half Marathons are conquered with timings being better every time and the last one was 2 hours and 2 minutes which is 15 minutes better than that of my first run of SCMM 2015. I knew that my next run could be a full marathon of 42.195 kilometers. Some of the experienced runners advised me to wait longer before doing a full marathon. There came the pop-up in my Facebook account regarding the trail run and the Mount Abu Trail Half Marathon was to be the next destination. It was a cold morning in the month of March, 2016 and I was on the starting line of the Mount Abu Trail Half Marathon in front of the Head Office of the Brahma Kumaris. The thought of a jungle trail which I had never seen before was really haunting me. The run started through the rolling slopes of the Mount Abu town after a semicircle around the famous lake and after 5 kilometers, we were into the Jungle Trail. I completed a tough trail half marathon in 2 hours and 15 minutes. That was a challenging and unique experience.

It is fact that your passion will always throw challenges at you and you will enjoy more and gain more from such challenges. The avenues other than your passion will also throw challenges at you and with effort you successfully overcome them but you may not enjoy success in the true sense.

The steps become tougher and the passion becomes stronger...

(d) What are the backups?

While following your passion at a late age, you start living in a different world altogether. It is my experience that I was fully occupied with the thoughts of running, plans of running, and my next running events. There was a danger of neglecting my job which was giving me a living. This is the danger when you follow your passion at a late age and you know pretty well that this could not replace your earning activity. This calls for a conscious effort to keep a balance between the 2. The planning for both should be very meticulous. A reasonable amount of compromise is required. I was planning for an Ultra Marathon in Silvassa in February, 2016, and, in fact, registered for it, but an office event planned later clashed, and I had to skip the Ultra Marathon to be part of the office meeting.

The choice between passion and profession was a first incident for me. Though I decided in favor of profession, I consciously weighed the pros and cons of both. That's important as with a late-age surge of passion, you can't replace your paying job. Previously, it was office and office only; even important family functions were not considered.

(e) What is the detailed plan?

The clarity regarding the "new me" and "old me" has been becoming obvious in me. I was sure of changing me from the "circumstantial me" to a "planned me." I have explained how my passions gave way to the middle-class compulsions of having a job and earning a livelihood, having a social status, being a responsible husband, being a responsible son, and being a responsible father. All these were measured by the ability of purchasing the necessities and comforts. The easy way out was to do academically well, secure a white-collar job and climb up the ladder in the organization to be a success. There was another way that was suppressed in me, i.e., following my passion and getting to fulfill all my responsibilities through it. This could have been done had I followed my passion right from a young age. Now at 50+, I can't do it to earn my livelihood. The fact is that I have earned reasonably well and have stability and I can live a part of my time meaningfully. That's the plan I have. I will pursue my passion as an amateur and still pursue my profession. As a matter of fact, I have decided to run 100 marathons by the time I turn 60 years of age and of those, 30 should be full marathons. By the time this book hits the book stands, I will have run 45 races with a few Full Marathons and Ultra Marathons. This plan included only one passion of mine, i.e., sports. What about writing, my other childhood passion? That's what I am doing now. The plan is clear. Amateur runner and writer.

I am very confident that these 2 will gift me a "New ME".

You too can plan a "New YOU".

CHAPTER 7
Only 20 km More... I was Excited...

The last 10 km stretch was tough with tired legs and setting a faster timing. I had consciously increased my cadence to 175, keeping the stride length the same as before. The idea of an injury-free run always has a high cadence and shorter stride length. That helped me to maintain the desired pace over the last 10 km segment. The break this time was a very short 2 minutes. The next 20 km needs to be covered in 2 hours and 22 minutes. That amounts to running the next 2 segments in around 70 minutes each, and the next break should be of 2 minutes only. My body and mind were in unison and I was about to revise the finishing time to more than 10 hours. I took some food and energy drink from my backpack, and quickly got ready to start the next leg. It is said when one door closes on you another opens. I heard a voice I recognized from behind me. A running buddy of many runs was approaching. He was a veteran of many ultra runs. He, while running along with me, appreciated my maiden effort so far and told me that I had a chance of finishing under 10 hours. Though I did not agree with him, I kept pace with him.. I considered him as my pacer for the next 10 km. During a long run if you choose to run in group, you tend to do better. He was bit faster. I followed him over the next 2 kilometers. I had the attitude of "never quit." Besides the vision of crossing over the finish line with a sub-10 timing, a smile and hug from my better half—she had already reached the finish line along with my son—was a strong motivation. The mind won, and I got into the pace my friend was setting and continued. The subconscious again took over sending me back into memory lane…

Into Running Races and Deep into the First Passion

The First Gift

(a) **What does my passion mean to me?**

Each individual, either consciously or unconsciously, has gifted something to himself by taking part in various activities. I have expressed my childhood passion at the start of this book. However, until I turned 50, I didn't do anything to follow my passion. The reasons may or may not have been in my control then. Had I followed my passion right from those days, I would have been a different individual. Now, at this stage of life, if I revive my passion, I will feel the happiness which I have never felt in my working life. This may give me some recognition that I crave for.

I decided to follow my passion for sports, and gift myself my passion once again after 4 decades. I took to running long distances in organized races where a fee is required to participate. Every time I stood on the starting line of a marathon, the number of known faces increased. The hugs and handshakes at the finish line also increased. Through this gift of passion, I gifted myself an array of friends from various walks of life. My mental horizon expanded beyond the insurance industry.

The urge to do more in long-distance running became stronger and stronger.

(b) My achievements for my family

Every time I come back from an organized race with a finishers' medal, I get a hero's welcome from my family. Invariably, I thank my wife by putting the medal around her neck. The happiness in doing that is inexplicable. In my working carrier, such moments were there when I got a promotion once in 2 or 3 years, but it was not frequent. In a short span of 3 years of long-distance running I have experienced this happiness 32 times so far. There have been a few times when my family has traveled to the marathon finish line to meet me.

(c) My journey through my first passion

In this section I would like to take my readers through the learning of various events I have participated in so far. Each of the 32 events (up to November, 2017) has taught me something new.

SCMM 2015

This is the first time I participated in January, 2015. Being the premier marathon event in India, this event holds a special position in the heart of an Indian marathoner. Oblivious to this fact, I set out to the venue in a pair of tracks and a t-shirt carrying the bib early in the morning. After reaching the start point, I had to ask somebody to pin the bib to my t-shirt. This means I was not well-prepared. The first lesson - be prepared in all aspects. I was wearing new shoes and this is also not correct as you should not run a race in shoes without proper practice. After the start, I ran the first 5 kilometers with a pace of 5.30 minutes per kilometer, but thereafter could not keep up the pace and had to toggle between running and walking the rest of the distance. After the first 13 to 14 km, there was an elevation to be climbed and this came as a surprise to me when my entire energy had depleted. Considering the fact that I had not studied the route and had not planned the pace, I felt that I didn't do justice to the race. With a little bit of difficulty, I completed the race in 2 hours and 17 minutes. In spite of being unprepared, the happiness at the finish line was immense. It can only be understood by one who has felt it himself.

Hiranandani Thane Half Marathon

This was my second run a month after the first one. This time, before the race day, I studied the route and its elevation profile, and planned the pace accordingly. I did not toggle between running and walking this time. The entire distance was covered with a pre-decided pace and completed in 2 hours and 11 minutes. I learned from this race to maintain a pre-decided pace over the various stretches of the route considering the elevation profile of each section. I neglected to consider the distance the elevation occurred. An elevation that comes after the first kilometer can be covered with a better pace than when it comes after 18 kilometers. I encountered this in HTHM.

Shriram Properties Bengaluru Marathon

After a long gap of around 7 months, I ran the third half marathon at Bangalore in September, 2015. This one taught me the importance of proper hydration and rest/sleep before the marathon. This was due to the humid Bangalore air that day. Though I completed the run in 2 hours 10 minutes, I was not comfortable during the entire run due to humidity and lack of sleep the previous night.

Airtel Delhi Half Marathon

It was November, 2015 and a cooler Delhi. The track was flat. The hydration was taken care of. Sleep was ample. The run went as planned and I completed the race in 2 hours and 4 minutes. For my age, it was a respectable time and I enjoyed the run.

Pune International Marathon (Half Marathon)

This was the last run of 2015, exactly a week after the Delhi event. By this time, I was aware of a few tricks of running long distances, and in spite of a few rolling elevations on the route, I had a good run and completed the race in 2 hours & 2 minutes.

Few things I learned from my first 5 half marathons:

1. Study the route and plan the pace
2. Study the weather, plan your hydration, rest, and sleep
3. Use proper running gear

The lessons were learned quickly because it was my passion, and I was enjoying the difficulties I faced in each of the events.

What Is New in Long-distance Running?

My passion for long-distance running has become an addiction by this time. The urge to do a few variations was stronger now. That led me to participate in a trail half marathon at Mount Abu in the month of March, 2016. The learning from a trail run was immense:

1. Keep a controlled pace
2. Keep an eye on foot landing while running
3. Be careful of tripping on the trail

Run-Up to a Full Marathon

The urge to try a tougher run led to running a 25 km route in Sanjay Gandhi National Park that involved 4 steep hills. This again taught me some new things:

1. How to climb uphill with shorter strides, lean forward and upper-cut arm movements.
2. How to run downhill keeping the knees injury-free.

The distance increased from 25 km to 32 km in a jungle run at Durshet Forest. My addiction to running was at a peak by August, 2016 when I was promoted and was transferred to Bhubaneswar. In spite of the hectic work schedule at Bhubaneswar, I continued to practice and increased my monthly mileage to 250+ km on a regular basis. This time the target was to run a full marathon of 42.195 km at the SCMM 2017.

SCMM 2017 (Full Marathon)

Running a full marathon is really meditation in motion. If you do not keep everything under control during a full marathon you will falter. All the experiences of HM, 25 km Endurathon, 32 km Jungle Run and Trail run proved immensely useful during my maiden Full Marathon in January, 2017.

I planned each kilometer of the 42.195 km. The cadence per minute, the breathing synced with cadence, the heart-rate, and the energy supplements were all planned meticulously.

The target was set for 4 hours and 45 minutes. The initial comfortable start, the middle portion speed, the hitting of the wall at 32 km and the final dash to the finish, all went well, and I finished in 4 hours & 46 minutes. The sense of becoming a marathoner gave me satisfaction. While posing for a photograph with the medal, I was really thanking myself for following my passion. I really gifted myself with the passion for running in the form of this medal in the FM category at SCMM 2017. The appreciation from the running community this time was overwhelming. The appreciation from the office in the form of my running photo being given a place in the house magazine with words of appreciation was really motivating.

Sense of Fulfillment

A sense of fulfillment in terms of my personal agenda surged through me. So far, I was measuring my success in terms of a promotion, increments, and added power. These were all related to financial gain. What gave me an inexplicable happiness was an activity which did not bring me any financial gain.

My journey of my first passion brought a few new things into my life:

1. A discipline to get up early in the morning
2. Taking a regular morning run which kept me fit
3. I have eliminated ailments like BP and obesity.
4. It kept my sugar levels in absolute control.

5. I am an introvert and did not have many friends. This passion for running connected me to thousands of running buddies across the globe.

6. The recognition from accomplished runners around the circuit and also acknowledgment of being a role model for new runners in the running circuit.

By this time, I have the following finisher medals adorning my Medal Hanger:

Year 2015

1. SCMM 2015 Half Marathon: 2 hours 17 minutes
2. Hiranandani Thane Half Marathon 2015: 2 hours 11 minutes
3. Shriram Properties Bengaluru Half Marathon: 2 hours 10 minutes
4. Airtel Delhi Half Marathon 2015: 2 hours 4 minutes
5. Pune International Half Marathon: 2 hours 2 minutes

Year 2016

6. Hiranandani Powai Half Marathon: 2 hours 2 minutes
7. SCMM 2016 Half Marathon: 2 hours 5 minutes
8. Our Marathon Pune (HM): 2 hours 2 minutes
9. Mount Abu Trail Half Marathon: 2 hours 15 minutes
10. TCS World 10 km Bengaluru: 57 minutes 22 Seconds

11. Last Sunday of June, Pune 15 km: 1 hour 28 minutes
12. BNP Endurathon 25 km: 2 hours 54 minutes
13. Last Sunday of July, Pune 15km (Ghat Run): 1 hour 44 minutes
14. Durshet Forest Marathon 32 km: 3 hours 54 minutes
15. IDBI Federal Mumbai Half Marathon: 2 hours 20 minutes
16. Tata Steel 25 km Kolkata: 2 hours 29 minutes

Year 2017
17. Tata Steel Bhubaneswar HM: 2 hours 9 minutes
18. SCMM Full Marathon: 4 hours 46 minutes
19. Last Sunday of May, Pune HM: 2 hours 12 minutes
20. Hope For Children Foundation HM, Pune: 2 hours 20 minutes
21. Last Sunday of June, Pune HM(Ghat Run): 2 hours 17 minutes
22. Mile Runners Half Marathon, Pune: 2 hours 3 minutes
23. Neo Vision HM, Pune: 2 hours 11 minutes
24. BNP Endurathon 25 km: 3 hours 6 minutes
25. Durshet Forest Marathon 32 km: 3 hours 43 minutes
26. IDBI Federal Mumbai Half Marathon: 2 hours 23 minutes

27. Run On Kharadi, 10 km Pune: 1 hour
28. PNB Metlife Satara Hill Half Marathon: 2 hours 11 minutes
29. Pune FLO Half Marathon: 2 hours 4 minutes
30. ICC Sinhagad 28 km Run: 3 Hours
31. Veterun Pune HM: 1 hour 59 minutes (My Personal Best)

These events have taught me many lessons which are comparable to a life journey. Each one of these runs was meditation in motion. The concentration, the focus, and the planning required to run the variety of events is mindboggling. If you are passionate, you can gather courage to face the challenges these events throw at you. You will be overwhelmed when you consider the number of participants and the very fact that you are not competing with any of them gives comfort. In fact, you only compete with yourself while running a marathon. The body and mind tug-of-war goes on for the entire distance, and the mind wins if you finish the race.

Every time I look at the medals in the hanger, I recount the meditation I did for each of them and the life lessons they have taught me. The emotions of despair and triumph are associated with each kilometer of tough uphill and downhill. Each of the triumphant 31 steps to the finish in the above races is the culmination of thousands of strides of determination and self-inflicted pain during each run.

All these gave me happiness in living my own passion.

I plan to run 100 races by the time I turn 60. This will include a few Ultra Marathons which involve a distance of more than 42.195 km. In fact, the Ultra Marathons require a tougher determination, tougher physical health, and better techniques for running. I am confident that I will do it. Of course, I am sure of strong support from my family.

I am extremely happy that I lived my first passion over the last 3 years and it gifted a new "ME" to me.

CHAPTER 8
Final Sprint to Realization of My Dream

The last 10 km with my running buddy was really a life lesson. When the end is well-defined and motivating, you tend to stretch beyond your comfort zone. The feeling was, "I have done so much, and I will not give up. I will push myself and realize my dream." To my surprise, the segment was completed in 65 minutes. The sense of accomplishment of a sub-10 finish was looming even though another 10 km was to be conquered. The need for more energy for the body was at its peak, but, my mental energy was increasing. I took an energy drink at the aid station from the smiling volunteers and decided not to take a break there as my buddy was continuing his run and had gone a little ahead of me. The pace of my feet increased as I set out to catch up with my buddy. Within few minutes I caught up with him, and I felt an energy surge to pull ahead of him. The encouragement from him was enough for me to increase my cadence, and I surged past him. The running community is really a wonderful lot. Each runner encourages the other with an attitude of selflessness. The last leg of the race is on and each kilometer was getting conquered by my striding feet. I got into my subconscious once again....

The Journey of Putting the Experience in Black & White

The Second Gift

(a) My Other Passion

During my formative years in school, one more thing had attracted my mind and that was communication through writing. One big attempt with my class mates and teachers was to publish a handwritten school magazine. The setback in doing this discouraged me and that passion was suppressed. I would not say it was nipped in the bud as my Head Master allowed those writings to be published in the form of a wall magazine. However, the fact that my article, which was a critique, didn't find a place in the wall magazine was a mental blow. During my university days, I was given the responsibility of designing the wall magazine of the Department of Analytical & Applied Economics. That was at a time when the necessity of doing well academically and getting a well-paying job was more intense than reviving my passion for writing. I fulfilled the duty assigned to me in a reasonable manner instead of going deeper into the assignment.

(b) The Attempts

My passion for writing had been all but obliterated. The rat race for position, good pay, and regular career enhancement has taken me at least 3 decades away from my passion of writing. I was at Lucknow and working as an area sales manager in the Corporate Business department. It was Monday, and I had just arrived at my office from a very hectic week tour through Bihar and Jharkhand. The office boy came to me with a parcel. The handwriting on the package was very familiar to me and, after opening it, I found it was from a very close friend of mine. It was a book written by a famous author with a note from my friend that said "Read it and you will identify yourself in some portion of the book." I read it and identified my initial days at Chennai. The book triggered the old suppressed passion in me and I thought of writing a book.

I started to write a fiction work based on my life experiences. On the first day, I wrote the introductory 3 pages. I shared this with my wife and my friend who gifted me the book. Both appreciated the idea and the initial start. However, the pressure of achieving sales numbers and the associated activities and mental stress of my job relegated the attempt to write a book into oblivion. I have kept those 3 pages and I am promising myself that one day I will finish it and bring it to my readers.

(c) The Incidents

This is the second time in this book that I am talking about an incident. I do believe that many of the twists and turns in one's life are the result of some incidents. As they say, a difficult catch taken in cricket can be the turning point for the match. In my case, there were few incidents that happened, and ultimately, I am on my laptop writing this book. The first incident was due to a family compulsion (which I can't explain in detail in this book). I decided to take a sabbatical leave for one year and stay at Pune. Initially, seniors in my company were reluctant to allow me to do this, but after giving me a hearing, my request was accepted. I was allowed to go on sabbatical for one year. Though my presence was required by my family at Pune, it was not required 24 hours of the day. After attending to some of the required activities, I had some spare time.

In the first 3 months of my leave, I decided to give some more time to my running activity. I practiced more and was able to participate in a number of races. This is physical activity and my body has limits particularly when you are 53 years old. I was toying with a few ideas of doing a skill enhancement course.

Suddenly, one day I found a Facebook message from somebody not known to me inviting me to participate in a seminar, "How to write a book in 21 days". First, I ignored this message thinking that it was junk message. After 2 or 3 days, I received the message again, and this time it offered a free registration and the venue was very close to where I was staying at Pune. This message rekindled my passion for writing. Out of curiosity, I registered for the free seminar. However, there was a clash of dates with one of my running events. I was supposed to be present at the seminar at 9 am sharp, and my running event would be over by 8 am. This was a nice conflict to have between my first passion and second passion. Obviously, I was almost living my first passion then and the decision was tilted in favor of running the race and sacrificing the seminar which was an unknown event. With this tug-of-war in mind, at one point I felt that with little bit of effort, I could do both. I decided to do the 10 km run that started at 6 am, finish the run within one hour, rush back home, then go to the seminar. I ran the 10 km in exactly 60 minutes, and a runner buddy gave me lift to my home and I was at the seminar just in time.

The seminar was addressed by an astute speaker who was thorough on the subject. He was speaking about the motivation, the processes, and the plans behind book-writing and publication.

At the end of his talk, he also showed a brief plan for writing a book which appealed to me a lot, and it was a take-away for me from that meeting.

These are the 2 incidents that triggered my suppressed passion for writing. The lesson from this is that you need to help your passion to come out of hibernation at the right opportunity. I thank God that I did it.

(d) Meeting the Angels

I came back from the seminar and was thinking, "Do I need to spend money and go for self-publishing my book? Is it worth doing?" It was Minati, my wife, who, after listening to the entire incident, really pushed me. She carefully went through the concept, the book plan, and the entire process of self-publishing a book. Her support was so much that it was an easy decision for me.

I called the speaker of that seminar and discussed the concept, my plan for the book, and the timelines. He was very supportive, suggested a few important things, and encouraged me to start writing. One important tip from him was, "Never read whatever you have written unless you have finished your book." He advised me to read and review the contents after I wrote the final chapter of the book. This activity is one of the important things that drive you to the completion of the book-writing.

Thus, I met an angel in the speaker and I also had my wife, the angel in my life for the last 24 years who is always by my side through thick and thin.

Friends, God sends angels to those who are honest and sincere. I don't know whether I was sincere in all aspects of my life, but I am sure I was and am sincere regarding my 2 passions, running and writing.

(e) The Support from My Better Half

Not only was the decision to write the book, but also the content of the book and the entire plan for writing the book was due to my wife's continuous support. She was there with me right from the beginning, from asking me to sit down to begin writing to switching the AC on and providing cups of tea. The assurance from her to read the manuscript before submission was very comforting because she is very candid and will give her opinion even in the form of a criticism.

I started to plan the book. In 2010 when I attempted a book, I was thinking of writing a work of fiction. The dilemma was choosing fiction or a non-fiction. After a thorough discussion with my publisher, I decided to choose my experience-based non-fiction. I am convinced of the fact that I will be candid about the life of an average middle-class individual and if read in the right perspective, each reader will be able to identify with some of the facts presented in this book.

The book-writing plan, as I understand now, was just a symbol of sincerity toward a timely finish of the book. The experience of writing a book is a synonym for running a full marathon. In a full marathon, a runner plans the start, the pace, hydration along the route, the uphill run, the turn-around, the downhill run, hitting the wall, the countdown to the finish line, and passing the finish line. In the true sense of a marathoner, I will also take you all through my book-writing journey with the plan of a marathon:

(i) The Start

I planned the book with my publisher. I prepared one page covering the entire plan of the book with all the areas I will be covering. The target group of readers was kept in mind while I decided to present my life experiences. The progress of the book was kept simple and slow as I normally do in starting a marathon.

(ii) The Pace

The pace of writing was decided to be slow. Gradually, as the stages of my life progress to various levels, the pace increases just like a marathon where the pace picks up after few kilometers.

(iii) Hydration Along the Route

During a marathon you need to replenish the loss of water and salt content in your body by sipping in water and energy drinks at regular intervals. Similarly, I decided to sit back and think, read a few materials, and travel down my memory lane to replenish the ideas and thoughts relating to my life and choose the facts that I would try to present to my readers.

(iv) The Uphill Run

During a marathon, you will come across elevations to be conquered, and they are the tough portions of the journey.

This requires a lot of determination and commitment. Similarly, there were times in writing this book when I felt that it was difficult to present what I intended. The ideas and vocabulary are not enough to impress the readers. Determination and commitment kept me going, just as it happens to me while negotiating those steep gradients in a marathon.

(v) The Turn-Around

Generally, in a marathon, the runners are required to go out and come back from the midpoint. The turn-around point gives a comforting feeling that half the distance is covered, and the countdown has started. The same thing happened to me when I finished a chapter "The First Gift". From there, it is just a countdown to the end as the second gift to me is getting this book published.

(vi) The Downhill

This section of the marathon route is generally less taxing as far as your muscles and lungs are concerned. There is a note of caution in each marathoner's mind not to overdo things while running down the gradient. This may hurt the knees. There is more chance of tripping because of the increased pace. Similarly, there are sections of the book which were easy for me to write, such as my experience with various marathons. I had to use a little more caution while writing that portion – providing details yet keeping it short and to the point.

(vii) Hitting the Wall

Every marathoner will agree with the fact that at around the 32-kilometer mark in a marathon, the runner hits the wall. At this point, the runner is out of energy and stamina to proceed further. The battle between the body and mind is at a peak. The body says "No", and the mind's voice becomes feeble with a mild "Yes". The marathoner tries to overcome the body's call and keeps going. Once the runner overcomes this with determination and grit, the rest of the journey to the finish line continues. There was a similar phase while writing this book. The feeling was that I had run out of ideas and vocabulary, and I was not including the kind of facts I wanted. I kept on with the true spirit of a marathoner and was determined and committed to present the facts of my experiences of following my passions of running and writing. That helped me to pass "hitting the wall" and proceed.

(viii) The Countdown to the Finish Line

During the course of a marathon, you come across the roadside sign boards stating 1000 meters to the Finish Line, 500 Meters to the Finish Line, and so on... This increases a runner's confidence to make it a memorable finish. A similar feeling crept over me while I was writing this portion of the book. The book plan shows me that I am at the last phase of writing my book. My sense of confidence has grown, and I am striding away toward the last phase of the book.

(ix) Passing the Finish Line

The flashing cameras, the cheering crowd, and the visibility of the finish line are a few things the marathoner meditates on during that 42.195 km grind, and once those are visible, the joys of achievement are endless. The marathoner feels at the top of the world. He thanks himself for putting in those grinding hours and holds the finisher's medal with pride. In this book-writing, I am near the finishing line, and the joys of reaching the finishing line are visible.

I am holding the medal, i.e. The Book, with pride, but there is a difference; the flashing cameras and cheering crowd on the finish line are not there. They are imaginary for me at this stage. I thank all those imaginary cheering crowds and flashing cameramen from the bottom of my heart.

The fact that I have gifted myself my 2nd passion i.e. the Book today will give me ample satisfaction. This satisfaction will multiply if I could encourage even one person to pursue his/her passion and get the happiness of gifting himself/herself a "New HIM/HER."

CHAPTER 9
The Finish Line of the Dream Ultra Marathon

"The last kilometer to the finish line. You have done it. Keep going…" reads the signboard. I came back to consciousness. I took a cursory glance at my Garmin. It showed 60 minutes for the last 9 km. That means I was bang on time for an under 10 finish. The cadence increased automatically. Always, during my previous runs, I got excited when the race was at the last kilometer. The urge to finish strong allows extra adrenaline into the system. Even after a grind of 74 kilometers, the urge for a strong finish made me sprint. The sight of my wife and my son taking pictures and videotaping the finishing sprint was another source of motivation to finish strong. For the first time, I saw my son getting excited in a sporting event and he ran along with me for the last kilometer taking the pictures and videos. The billboard showed 100 meters to the finish, and the finishing gate was in sight. The feeling of ecstasy was setting into my mind. The visualization of the medal around my neck was flashing past my mind's eye. I crossed the finish line and stopped the Garmin, which had almost run out of power as it was tracking the run for last 10 hours. It was a sub-10 finish. The hug from my wife and my son were the real prizes at that point. The organizers were kind enough to garland the medal right at the finish line. It took some time to sink in. I had run the Ultra Marathon- a dream I nurtured for the last 3 years. Tears of joy were rolling down my cheeks.

I was brought back to reality when my son told me, "Papa, it seems we have reached the starting point of the race at Loni Kalbhor." The journey from my home at Pune to this place started very early in the morning. My son was driving, and I was having a nap for an hour during which I dreamed of the entire run which I was going to run that morning. I left the car and proceeded toward the start line of my life's first Ultra Marathon.

THE BIG DREAM vs. THE REAL ULTRA RUN (Pune Ultra Run 2017)

I will be failing in my duty if don't narrate my real experience of my first Ultra Marathon versus the dream which I had during that car ride to reach the starting line of the Pune Ultra Marathon. The following section is my real experience of my first Ultra Marathon, which is a dream come true for me.

Preparations

After 4 months of training for this Ultra Marathon of 75 km—the first ultra for me—D-day was just a day away. I had kept the previous day as a rest day. No running and only few minutes of stretching in the morning. I was stressed because of the apprehension of running 75 km. It would be a ten-hour grind.

I had read about the various segments of the route, the elevations, and trails, but I had never seen or experienced it. I chalked out my plan for the route: the segments which I would run, the segments which would be walked, and the segments which would increase the average pace, and keeping in view the cut-offs. The race had 2 cut-off segments: the first 33 km in 4 hours, the next 25 km in the next 4 hours, and overall finish within 11 hours. For a novice like me, it surely looked daunting, but it might not have intimidated the experienced runners.

During, the training—self-training, without a coach—I had practiced long runs at an average pace of 07:30/km and was very confident that I could maintain this pace for quite a long-distance. I had not run any distance beyond 30 km during the training. My longest distance so far was 42.2 km in SCMM 2017.

After all preparations were done, we had an early dinner, and went to bed around 9 pm. We got up at around 03:30 am started for the venue at 04:00 am as we were to report before 04:30 am at the venue. My wife agreed to accompany me to the venue which is 16 km away from my residence at Pune.

The Google Maps voice said, "Turn left in 200 meters, and your destination will be on the left."

We saw only one vehicle parked outside the Innovera School gate. My wife was a bit apprehensive. "Have we reached the venue?" I was sure of the place and this had happened before for some of my last running events where I had reached the venue early. After parking the car, we went into the school and found the organizers offering hot tea, which was most welcome in that chilly weather. A few participants were also there. Out-station runners were housed in the school and slowly the meeting with running buddies and interactions began. We collected the bib in the meantime. The organizers announced that the briefing about the race would be at 05:30 am and the race will be flagged off at 6.

With a total of 38 runners and 4 pacers, of all categories: 75 km, 100 km, and 100 miles, the run was flagged off at 06:00 am while it was still dark.

The route was 12.5 km out and back so one loop was 25 km. This distance and route had to be conquered 3 times. The 12.5 km consisted of:

1. 3 km of tar
2. 2 km of mud along a canal

3. 3 km of tar with elevations

4. 4.5 km of unforgiving tough trail

Loop 1

The first 3K of the route was dark and infested with stray dogs. Seeing crazy creatures running in the dark caused obvious reactions from the stray dogs and few of them tried to attack. Just after 2 km, one such dog came running toward me violently and I tripped while avoiding it. I had a bad fall, but fortunately I escaped unhurt except for a bruise on my right palm. I continued my run though I was bleeding from my palm. I needed to be careful along the canal on the mud road and, in the meantime, daylight broke and the road was visible. I reached the first-aid station at the 5 km mark and received first-aid for the wound and took some water. The volunteer angels were so caring that I immediately recollected the statement from Sangeeta Lalwani, one of the organizing members, who said "You will be surprised by the pampering by the volunteers." It was really a surprise and kudos to the Free Runners Group.

From there to the Ramdhara Temple aid station was a tar road with 4 inclines to be negotiated. Out of the 4, 3 were moderate and did not pose any problem. But one incline, the second one from the last aid station, was really tough. My fresh legs and the cool morning atmosphere helped me to run up the inclines without much trouble.

While climbing, I was thinking these inclines would be tough to negotiate in the second and third loops. I reached the Ramdhara Temple aid station after circling around the temple pond and the volunteers welcomed me with claps; the treatment was amazing. That was 8 km from the start.

After recording the timing there, the trail of 4.5 km started. While getting into the trail, I met fellow runner Stephen Walker who was from London. It was nice talking to him and I tried to maintain his pace. He told that he had done a 100-mile race in 16 hours in July. Obviously, as a novice to ultra-running, I was finding it difficult to keep pace with him on a very difficult and uneven trail. Somehow I maintained his pace through the trail. Just at the end of the trail there was the turn-around aid station. We were welcomed as heroes by the aid station volunteers.

Photographs were taken, timing was recorded, and after the water and energy replenishments, we started back. By that time, we had used 1 hour and 12 minutes. Considering the difficulty level of the route it was good timing, but Stephen was in no mood to relent. He increased his pace and I began to lag behind. I decided to keep my pace and complete the first loop of 25 km under 2.5 hours. The atmosphere was cool then and the trail did not pose any problem. Considering the fall I had, I was more conscious of my steps lest I would trip. There were a few farmers' lands along the trail that were cultivated with vegetables like tomatoes and beans. Mostly, the trail had a deserted look. I was wondering what would happen if I required help in an emergency, but to my relief, I saw volunteers patrolling the route on motorcycles. I waved at them, they smiled, and I moved on toward the Ramdhara Temple aid station. As usual, the volunteers gave me a warm welcome. This time along with water, energy drinks, salts and Jhagri, Mr. Parag Dongre offered a massage of calf muscles, and sponged my neck and head. That was real pampering. Time to move on.

Starting again with refreshed legs, it was mostly downhill to the 5 km mark aid station near the canal. As per my plan, this portion of the route was for a faster pace, but I decided to keep a pace that would not hurt my knees on the descent. By the time I reached the aid station, I had used 1 hour and 50 minutes and I felt that I was on time for my first loop.

I cut my break short and started toward the starting point at the Innovera School to complete the first loop. The run along the canal on the muddy road was tricky as there was a possibility of tripping. By the time I entered the school, my Garmin was showing 02:27. I was on time as per my plan. The fresh legs, cool weather, and initial excitement of running the ultra got me through the first loop, and I had enough time to hit the 33 km cut-off well within time.

The volunteers at the start/finish aid station clapped and the timing was recorded. The sponging of neck, legs, and head was done. Water and energy replenishments were taken. Seeing my wife at the starting line was an added comforting factor. She was enquiring whether I was okay to continue the run. The concerns were valid when she saw the bruise on my palm. I assured her that I would listen to my body and if I needed to pull back I would do so. The organizers offered breakfast, but I preferred a banana and egg whites.

Loop 2

I started for the second loop, and more importantly to hit the first cut-off point at Ramdhara Temple aid station. I had 1 hour and 28 minutes to reach the cut-off point. I decided to keep a comfortable pace of around 7 minutes/km to reach the cut-off point in 30 minutes. The angel volunteers at the Canal Road aid station informed me while recording the timing that I was number 2 in the 75 km category so far.

After the usual pampering, I left for the cut-off point which was 3 km away, having allowed 55 minutes to get there. This was a very comforting factor and I thought even if on tired legs, I can maintain a pace of 7 minutes/km and reach the Ramdhara Temple aid station in next 25 minutes. Climbing the inclines posed a few issues to my tired legs, but I told myself, "Hey you can't complain of tired legs. Run from your core. You have one more lap to go." As per my plan, I reached the cut-off point and recorded the time. I was 32 minutes ahead of time. The volunteers sponged and massaged my legs. The sunshine in this loop was little harsh on the runners.

According to my plan, I was required to cover the next 25 km in 4 hours and I had 4 hours and 30 minutes as I saved some time from the first cut-off. I started from the Ramdhara Temple and proceeded into the trail which was looking harsher due to the sun shining brightly. Having the company of an accomplished Ultra Marathoner, Mr. Sukanto Roy, on this segment was a help as I could maintain a rhythm alongside him. A lots of things regarding ultra-running could be learned from him. This segment of 4.5 km to the next aid station at the turn-around was managed with a slow but steady pace. I reached the turn-around and the consistent support from the aid station was amazing. All the volunteers were as if God sent angels to me.

Time for the turn-around and on the return along with Sukanto, I picked up the company of another celebrity runner, Ms. Taru Mateti. She was running in the 100 km category. Three ultra-runners: Taru for 100 km, Sukanto for 161 km, and me for 75 km, took up a rhythmic pace toward the Ramdhara Temple through the harsh trail. We reached the Ramdhara Temple aid station. The volunteers lead by Prasad Dongre, popularly known as PD, took good care of us. PD advised me to take more salt as he saw the salt marks on my tee and shorts. The experience of PD who ran the 100 miler on this route before was really coming in handy through his advice to the runners and particularly novices like me.

Taru, Sukanto, and I started from the Ramdhara Temple and I was thinking about the fact that I am setting my foot beyond the full marathon distance for the first time. After another 8 km from there, I would complete my first 50 km run. I thought the rolling elevation from Ramdhara Temple to the aid station at Canal Road would not be a challenge, but as we proceeded, I found myself lagging behind Taru and Sukanto. I decided not to push myself to keep their pace. I kept myself in my comfort zone and reached the Canal Road aid station only 5 minutes after them. At the aid station, the sponge, massage, water, and energy supplements were in abundance. While recording the timing, the volunteers informed that I am second in my category.

The next 5 km to the base station at the school was along the canal and the road through Loni Village. I was feeling a little tough due to depleting energy and tired legs. But the thought of covering the third loop was keeping me going and I finally reached the aid station at the Innovera School just after 6 hours from the start of the race, i.e. at 12 noon and 50 km. The volunteers at the aid station took good care with sincere attention to the minute details of the requirements of a runner after a 50 km run. The lunch was in order and my wife came up with bananas and energy drinks.

Loop 3

I took 2 bananas and some energy drinks and started out at around 12:05 toward the next cut-off point with the goal of 1 hour and 55 minutes. I decided to cover the next 8 km in 1 hour and 10 minutes. Things went as per plan and with a break of a few minutes at the Canal Road aid station, I was on the way toward the Ramdhara Temple. This segment of the route looked like a solo run as no one was visible in front or behind me. While climbing the steep elevation, Sangeeta Lalwani cheered me from her car while she passed me. I reached the Ramdhara Temple aid station, the final cut-off point, at 01:15 pm, which was well ahead of the 2 pm deadline I had set. I had 45 minutes on hand.

I had completed 58 km. For next 17 km, I had 3 hours and 45 minutes to complete it within the cut-off time of 5 pm. I was aiming for a sub-10-hours finish, so now I had 2 hours and 45 minutes. The next 4.5 km to the turn-around point aid station is the trail with lots of ups and downs with a very uneven surface for running. My depleted energy levels and tired legs were a bit of a challenge, but my mind was determined. I calculated I had 165 minutes to cover 17K and it was looking easy. But I tell you, it was not as easy as the arithmetic involved. I reached the turn-around after running 4.5 km in 40 minutes.

I started the final return toward the Ramdhara Temple with a feeling that the home loop was in sight. Another

45 minutes, and I was checking into the Ramdhara aid station. On the way, a running buddy from Pune, Yogesh Almale, asked me to pose for a photo. While recording my arrival at Ramdhara, the volunteers informed me that I was in second position. This information gave me a good feeling and charged me up for the last 8 km. I had 80 minutes to cover the next 8 km. After the regular dose of water, salt, and energy drink, I started off from the aid station. As it was the last visit to the aid station, I took time to thank all the angels there and took the pond side road toward the Canal Road aid station which was 3 km away. This segment did not pose a challenge as it was mostly downhill with a little climb in the beginning.

Ace runner Taru Mateti was ahead of me and within visual range. She was running the 100 km. She had another loop to do. A comforting feeling came over me while I compared her run with mine as this was my last loop. After 25 minutes, I reached the Canal Road aid station. The volunteers greeted me with a standing ovation. I could not guess the reason. They informed me that the first runner was just 7 minutes ahead of me. They encouraged me to go fast and catch up with him. But my body was not up to it after a 70 km run. Next 5 km needed to be completed in 55 minutes to achieve my goal of a sub-10-hour finish. I stayed with my goal.

The road along the canal toward the base station looked longer this time. The fight between the body and mind was at its peak. The mind was confident, but the body was pulling back. The clever mind started visualizing the finish line and the feelings of completing my first Ultra Marathon kept me preoccupied and ignoring the negativity from the body. Finally, the turn toward the finish line from the main road was in sight. The veteran of many ultras, Mr. Sukanto Roy, congratulated me as he passed me on his fourth loop. I turned into the Innovera School campus and suddenly heard a resounding applause from the base station volunteers and I felt ecstatic with a spring in my legs. I sprinted the last 100 meters as if I was trying to beat Usain Bolt. The sight of my wife Minati waiting at the finish line with a mixed feeling of anxiety and happiness was giving me a sense of extreme pleasure.

The aid station volunteers took good care of me and informed me that I have secured the second position though the race organizers had already declared all finishers as winners.

Finally, the Finisher's Memento was presented to me by another veteran of many ultras, Mr. Piyush Shah and Race Director, Mr. Badri.

The BIG DREAM to become an Ultra Marathoner was a reality now...

Epilogue

(a) Daily Solo Practice Runs in the Morning

I was a morning walker/jogger of 4 to 5 kilometers since 2004 when my childhood friend, Santosh, introduced me to my daily morning routine. Until 2015 when I ran the SCMM Half Marathon, I had not thought of extending my morning walk/jog to long-distance running.

Since then, I started my morning run which eventually extended to 20 kilometers during my stay at Mumbai. I would get up early in the morning at 4 am and hit the road at 4:30 am almost daily. Being an introvert by nature, I started running solo. During these solo runs of 2 to 3 hours in the morning, I had time exclusively for me allowing for calm introspection about myself and the situation I was in. Many of the unsolved problems of the job and my personal life found their solutions during the meditation in motion and the solitude it provided to me.

There are many occasions when I would come back from my morning run and jot down the solutions to many pending problems and then acted on the same. To my surprise, those solutions worked wonderfully well.

The daily morning run became a part of my life and problem-solving time in addition to my fitness program. The change in my attitude to the various situations in my profession and personal life became visible.

(b) Running a Half Marathon

I informed my wife in the month of February, 2015 that I would not be coming to Pune from Mumbai during the second weekend of the month as I would be running the Hiranandani Thane Half Marathon, my second run after the SCMM 2015. The voice at other side of the phone was a little perplexed and wanted to know what I gained from my first Half Marathon run in January, 2015. It was a natural question from a non-runner. I had never shared the journey of my first HM from start to the finish with her except for putting the medal around her neck with pride.

I explained the entire journey to her as her support is indispensable if I wanted to take this passion further (I had decided already to do exactly that).

Why run the same distance again and again?

When I reached the starting line of SCMM 2015 on January 18, 2015, I was apprehensive about my ability to finish the race. I had never run that distance before. The crowd that gathered to run this distance was so huge that I was overwhelmed. The feeling of inferiority almost overwhelmed me seeing the way people were geared up, the intensity of their warm-ups, and technicalities being discussed among the participants. "Am I there?" I questioned myself.

The tug-of-war between my rational self and the runner in me continued. Finally, I decided that I would run and finish this distance. I wanted to live with my ignorance of the technicalities of running a Half Marathon for the next 2 to 3 hours and just put one foot in front of the other till I reached the finishing line. Sometimes, too much complexity deters you from starting something new.

While I was deep into these aspects, the crowd started moving toward the starting line. The crowd was so huge that before I realized, I had crossed the starting line and began jogging along with thousands of runners wearing every color possible. The movement with the colorful crowd continued for 2 kilometers. Every moment, a few runners were going ahead of me. At the 2 km mark, I felt that I was lagging behind almost everybody. The comforting factor was that I could see a sea of human beings behind me. That feeling just took me back to the advice of one of my professors during my university days. His advice was, "Whenever you feel that you are at a disadvantage, don't look up. Look down, and you will see there are people in a worse position than you."

Due to the initial euphoria of moving faster (by my standards), I felt like stopping and taking a breath at the 5 km mark. As a first timer, I was not comfortable stopping during a marathon and thought people would laugh at me. I was trying to push on even though I was out of breath, and my lungs were burning. Just at this point, we were at the Worli from the sea link and one angel from behind patted me and told me to take a water break, gather my breath, and start again. I still don't know who it was. He seemed to be a regular in the event and was cruising ahead of me. I followed his advice and took a water break, gathered my breath, and started again. The life lesson here was that each individual in the marathon between life and death have different capabilities and needs. We must respect that. The fellow runner respected it, and as an individual, I should have respected that instead of pushing on.

My energy level was depleting, and replenishments were being taken at the water stations and the rhythmic motion of one foot after another continued at a certain pace which I was not aware of. I reached the Pedder Road incline and the crowd on both sides of this road was awesome. They were cheering almost every step of each runner climbing the incline. Though I was not comfortable running up the incline, the cheering crowd did not allow me to walk. I ran up the incline to the rhythmic claps of the cheering crowd, and while going down the incline on the other side, I just remembered a poem which was taught to us during my school days, "Going Down the Hill on a Bicycle". The essence of the poem was that every hard time changes to a good one in a cycle.

At the Babulnath Turn, it was matter of 5 km more and the expectation of reaching the finish line became stronger. One person in the cheering crowd shouted to one of the runners, "You are doing well, and you are poised to finish at around 2:30." This statement, though directed to another runner, seemed applicable to me. I just felt motivated as I was never sure of completing the run. Now I am in time for a 2:30 finish. My cadence increased out of motivation and happiness. A new energy level ignited in me. In hindsight, I saw that the last 5 kilometers of my run were at a pace of 5:30minutes/km and I completed the run in 2:17:54. The status information at regular intervals helps and motivates for a better performance.

The tug-of-war experienced between the body and mind all through the race was an experience worth traversing. Facing unknown challenges and overcoming them was invaluable. The visible physicality of the activity is obvious, but there is a greater mental activity and this started (for me) from the second kilometer mark onwards to the finish line.

Now if this was the experience, I had gone through it. Then, why run one more?

The answers to this are:

1. I was addicted to the runner's high due to the endorphin secretion in the brain during the run.

The endorphin gives you a feeling of happiness and every runner is addicted to it.

2. The lessons I learned in the first one needed to be reinforced again and again so that it becomes a part of my spontaneous reaction to similar situations.

3. The routes of each marathon are different. They pose different challenges, and the runners need to face and overcome them. The same is a fact of life. Different challenges are posed at different stages of life.

Running the half marathon distance in various places and routes has taught me many lessons. Apart from the fact that I am following my passion, a journey in half marathons has converted me into an individual who has a new perspective of the turns and twists of life's journey. I am more composed, and now I am approaching every challenge in life more confidently as I negotiate those unknown challenges on my way to the finish line.

(c) Running a Full Marathon

It was July, 2016, and the registrations had opened for a full marathon for SCMM 2017. By that time, I had run 10 half marathons including a tough 25 km run involving 4 hill climbs. Also, I had registered for a 32 km Jungle Marathon scheduled for the first weekend of August, 2017. The instinct to explore the unknown was gaining ground in my mind amidst the fear. I logged onto the SCMM site and registered for the full marathon of SCMM 2017. This time, out of fear, I did not inform my wife about the full marathon.

In September, 2016, I was transferred to Bhubaneswar, but my family was staying at Pune. On January 12, 2017, I told my wife that I was to run the SCMM 2017 January 15 just like the last 2 years. I would come to Pune on January 12 and on the evening of January 14, I would go to Mumbai for the run the next day. The flight was direct from Mumbai to Bhubaneswar on the afternoon of January 15.

As planned, I ran the SCMM full marathon on January 15, 2017, rested at my colleague's house, and returned to the airport to catch the flight. Of course, immediately after the race, I had called my wife to inform her about the outcome, but she was not there. While checking into the airport, I got a call from her and she asked, "Why did you take so much time to finish your run this time?" The timing SMS had gone to her mobile and it was 4 hours 46 minutes and 03 seconds. I had to tell her that I ran the first full marathon of my life, and I am officially a marathoner. Her response was mixed. She wanted to know what the difference was except for the distance.

By that time, I had already planned for an Ultra Marathon toward the end of 2017, and now it is my responsibility to keep her by my side by explaining the difference and the necessity of running a full marathon.

Why a Full Marathon?

I agreed with her about running 42.195 km being crazy, madness etc. I empathized with her because I could understand the difference between a person who has done it, and one who has not. I had to convince her with sufficient logic what I have gained from such an activity as a person. Simply saying that I did it out of curiosity of the unknown will not break any ice with her.

Every individual feels that he/she is missing something in their life. When this feeling grows stronger, he/she goes out to face tough conditions, endure challenges, and accomplish something which he/she can be proud of. Nothing of this sort can be achieved without enduring pain. This gives the individual a feeling of accomplishing a heroic deed.

After the successful half marathons, the next challenge is full marathon. The very fact that I will have to do a HM twice on the same go was looking daunting. I have taken all the pains to go through the training despite a busy schedule of a high-pressure job and self-managing everything staying alone at Bhubaneswar. This shows that the urge to take my passion to the next level was strong enough and cannot be denied.

To go beyond the half marathon and reach the finish line of a full marathon teaches you one important thing; older order changes, yielding a place for the new. Any change requires a lot of dedication. The human instinct is always to choose tougher challenges. Had that not been the case, we would be running marathon distances for our daily share of food--maybe in the jungle killing prey or we would be running to save our lives from predators. It is just a tribute to those people who have decided to endure pain and who brought all the comforts of modern life to us.

Those who run full marathons are crazy but not crazier than those who challenged the status quo to provide new inventions and discoveries to mankind. Yes, running a full marathon gives a sense of victory over the mind and body which every individual wants but very few achieve. An attitude of "never quitting" is reinforced into the system of the runner every time he crosses the finish line of a full marathon.

I never knew that I could convince her about the logic of running a full marathon. I can proudly say that she has agreed to my Ultra Marathon plan in future.

(d) Writing a Book

Writing this book has been a unique experience. I have run 31 Marathons as of this date. The experience of running a race keeps me afloat for some time and then gets relegated to the background yielding a place for newer experiences in the future.

Writing this book has helped me relive all my experiences from my childhood through to this stage of my life. The summary of events this book has made me relive is:

1. Childhood experiences and the lessons learned
2. The compulsions that led me away from passions
3. The Individual that I am for my family, friends, and society.
4. The incidents that ignited my passions.
5. The experiences and lessons learned from passions.

The entire life-changing events of running long distances over the last 3 years, culminating in writing this book has changed many things within me.

Now I look at life in a more positive way.

I enjoy my association with everyone with lot of positivity.

My family and friends are seeing a happy me without any hypocrisy of pretended happiness.

In the process, didn't I gift myself a "New Me" wrapped in RUN?

I am sure YOU TOO CAN

www.ingramcontent.com/pod-product-compliance
Lightning Source LLC
Chambersburg PA
CBHW032144040426
42449CB00005B/395